AND I WILL GIVE YOU REST:

A 40-Day Self-Care Devotional Journal

This Journal Belongs To:

____

And I Will Give You Rest:
A 40-Day Self-Care Devotional Journal

by Jamie Coles Burnette, M.Div., M.A.

Unless otherwise noted, all Scripture quotations are taken from the **New King James Version** of the Bible.

Published 2024

Soul Sabbath Ministries

Int. Copyright: CI-36916410156

ISBN: 9798338209400

INTRODUCTION

Congratulations on accepting this 40-day Divine invitation into the journey and discipline of rest and self-care!

This devotional is primarily a call to experience the rest of God particularly through care of self. We are corporeal and incorporeal, which means that the visible and invisible parts of our being need ministering/tending to. One of the first images that we are presented with in Scripture is that of a garden, and humanity was charged with the responsibility of tending and keeping it. Following that imagery, you are a garden that needs tending and protecting.

INTRODUCTION

Why 40-days?

The Biblical witness highlights the number 40 in many ways. One of the most palpable connections is between the number 40 and the wilderness. We are reminded of ancient Israel's 40-year journey in the wilderness, as well as Jesus' time in the wilderness being tempted by The Adversary. Both of these experiences reflected times of self-discovery and exploring one's identity.

The wilderness was known to be a harsh place, where it would take strength, creativity, and fortitude to survive. So, too, during this journey you will be encouraged to face yourself: confront the growing edges and celebrate your strengths. With God's help, and your commitment to being the best you that you can be, you will learn and reflect on how to implement self-care as a spiritual discipline that will help you thrive in the wilderness and all seasons of life.

INTRODUCTION

Why a Journey?

Self-care is a journey, not a destination in and of itself. It is a road of new discoveries, recalibrations, and even course corrections. It is a means of learning how to release our tendencies towards control and lean into divine strength. This journey of self-care is a resource towards our ultimate destination, which is the shalom, or wholeness of God that encompasses our entire spiritual and material planes of being. Self-care is one of the ways we experience God's wholeness.

Why a Discipline?

Self-care and rest are also disciplines in that they are conscious, consistent, daily commitments to honor God by honoring and caring for the self.

It is my prayer that at the end of this 40-day journey, you will emerge with a greater sense of how beautifully you reflect the imago Dei (image of God), and resources of care that will inform and amplify your witness of The Way of Jesus Christ in your daily life.

INTRODUCTION

What to Expect

This devotional journal will provide meaningful, practical, faith-based reflections on self-care and rest, as well as opportunities for you to discover and wonder in a significant way about what self-care and rest looks like or needs to look like for you during this season in your life. The forces of evil are afraid of believers that are well-rested – not only in terms on sleep, but who are firmly at rest (anchored) in the God of their salvation! So always remember, the BEST you is a RESTED you!

As a devotional journal, there are some guided meditations/reflections to inspire and encourage you, and there are also guided prompts to assist you in reflecting, as well as ample space for you to write, reflect, and share your thoughts and even prayers in written form. You will also discover some devotional days will be less of a guided meditation, and more of an invitation into a particular self-care practice. Part of self-care is allowing your God-given creativity to flow. Allow the blank pages to be a canvas of ideas and wonderings born out of this intentional set-aside time with God and yourself.

INTRODUCTION

This book follows a weekly rhythm: mid-week (Wednesdays) you will be prompted to engage in listening to yourself: to slow down and pay attention to the signs and signals that your body and emotions are giving you. Saturdays you will be encouraged to engage in a particular self-care activity.

You may engage in the one included or feel free to do something of your choice that ministers/pours back into you. Sundays are days for you to look back and ahead: to reflect on your self-care journey over the previous week, think about what self-care may need to look like for you in the coming week, and plan for it.

Note that while this book has a weekly rhythm in mind, follow the weekly rhythm that works best for you. Maybe your mid-week check-in works better for you on another day of the week, and that's fine, too.

Blessings on your self-care journey!

~ Jamie

DATE / /

Day 1

(Sunday): "And I Will Give You Rest"

Thought for Today

"Come to me, all you who are weary and burdened, and I will give you rest. Take my yoke on you and learn from me, because I am gentle and humble in heart, and you will find rest for your souls. For my yoke is easy to bear, and my load is not hard to carry." (Matthew 11:28-30, NET)

The words of Jesus in Matthew 11 help us anchor our journey into wholeness through self-care. He issues one of the most beautiful, but challenging invitations to us who sometimes (or often) struggle with the application of self-care pillars such as rest, discipline, boundaries and more.

DATE / /

Day 1

(Sunday): "And I Will Give You Rest"

Thought for Today

Consider the beauty of Jesus' invitation:

- All the weary and burdened are invited. There are no prerequisites or degrees of weariness one has to reach to come to Jesus. But Jesus simply and beautifully recognizes the nuances of our human experience: there are some of us who need rest because of what we have been doing, and some of us need rest because of what we have been carrying, and sometimes because of both.

- And I will give you rest: Jesus emphasizes that rest is a gift. It is not something we have to earn, accrue, or be "good enough" to receive.

Also consider the challenge in accepting Jesus' invitation:

Also consider the challenge in accepting Jesus' invitation:

- **Come to me**. How many of us find it difficult to ask for help, or admit when we don't have it all together? In order to come to him, we will have to come face-to-fact with our frailties, weaknesses, and carefully crafted images, and admit that we need help. His invitation also reminds that we are to look to Him for our souls' refreshing and resist the temptation to seek solace in other places and enterprises that ultimately cannot satisfy.

DATE / /

Day 1

(Sunday): "And I Will Give You Rest"

Thought for Today

- **Take my yoke** on you and learn from me. In order to truly receive rest for our souls, it will require us to be humble and accountable (take the yoke), and learn from Jesus new ways of being, thinking, and doing. All of this will take us out of our comfort zones, and is not an overnight process, but a daily journey.

As you begin this journey, think about the areas of your life that you sense weariness and being burdened. Begin to commit these areas specifically to prayer and be open to the new ways of being, thinking, and doing that the Holy Spirit will lead you into in order to experience rest for body and soul.

MY REFLECTIONS

DATE / /

Day 2

(Monday): "It is Good": Resting from Perfectionism

Thought for Today

"And God saw everything that he had made, and behold, it was very good… 2 And on the seventh day God finished his work that he had done, and he rested on the seventh day from all his work that he had done."

(Genesis 1:31, 2:2, ESV)

I once heard a wise theologian say that God's rest after creating the world was not because God was tired, but God's resting signified that everything was complete. When a chef creates a dish, sprinkling and mixing seasonings to taste, when God said, "It is very good," it was a signal that creation was now "to taste" – *chef's kiss!*

Perhaps you've never experienced similar satisfaction because perfectionism never really allows anything in life to be "to taste." Perfectionism often robs us of joy and the peace that comes with not having to be in control of every single outcome. Perfectionism never allows us to truly rest at the moment, but it always hurries us on to the next thing or keeps us tinkering with a thing so we can make or keep it "perfect."

DATE / /

Day 2

(Monday): "It is Good": Resting from Perfectionism

Thought for Today

Genesis 1 teaches us that even God recognized when something was good enough or finished, and God took an intentional moment in time to honor that.

As a recovering perfectionist, especially as someone who wears multiple hats, I now realize that some days taste different than others, and so I have learned to give myself grace if the bed doesn't get made that day or there's a dirty dish in the sink, or my perfectly planned schedule for the day or timeline I set to accomplish certain things gets rerouted by the unexpected. Our worth isn't based on how perfectly we execute and deliver everything free of hiccups but on how faithful we are in and to the process God has laid out for us.

Now, this is not an excuse for laziness or for not trying your best, but it is an invitation to you to take a moment and celebrate where you are and enjoy your journey – to take a step back and say, "It," whatever your "it" is, is good.

To think about: What have you struggled to say "It is good" in your life? Is it something that legitimately needs work, or have you been putting undue pressure on yourself? Have you discerned God's mind about it in prayer and other spiritual disciplines (study, worship, fasting) to help you know the difference?

MY REFLECTIONS

DATE / /

Day 3

(Tuesday): The Power of "Yes!"

Thought for Today

"I am able to do all things through the one who strengthens me."
(Philippians 4:13, NET)

When is the last time you took the limits off yourself and gave yourself permission to soar?

Perhaps you grew up in an environment where you were consistently told "no." The "no's" may have been loud and glaring through statements like, "Who do you think you are?" or "No one in our family has ever done that before." The "no's" may also have come from more subtle signals and experiences that we deeply internalized such as a past failure, or even the fear of failing.

Part of self-care involves allowing ourselves to live fully into who God made us to be and what God has assigned us to do, which means that even when we experience what seems like a chorus of "no's," that we anchor ourselves in the "yes" from God, and the "yes" from ourselves, because if we are honest, there are some plans, projects, and pursuits that God has already placed in our hearts, but we have stood in our own way.

DATE / /

Day 3

(Tuesday): The Power of "Yes!"

Thought for Today

Begin to set aside some time to think about the areas of your life where you have "dimmed your light" and not allowed yourself to be free to live out loud and into your full God-given nature and purpose. Identify any traumatic or negative experiences, or internal barriers or negative self-talk that have contributed to any self-limitations or barriers to forward movement. Be kind to yourself in this process. Ask God to show you how to identify, confront, and overcome these limitations. If needed, consider enlisting the services of a professional therapist or counselor that can assist you with gaining tools and techniques to overcome these limitations and move forward.

MY REFLECTIONS

DAY: **4 (Wednesday)**

SELF-CARE CHECK-IN DAY

Self-Care Listening: How am I feeling today?

Are my body, mind/emotions giving me any signals that I need to slow down and pay attention to today?

DAY: **4 (Wednesday)**

SELF-CARE CHECK-IN DAY

How can I partner with God to give myself or receive the support I need?

How do I need to let others know how they can support me today?

MY REFLECTIONS

DATE / /

Day 5

(Thursday): Resting in Your God-Given Identity

Thought for Today

"And a voice came from heaven, 'You are my beloved Son; with you I am well pleased.'" (Mark 1:11, ESV)

I'm sure we have witnessed and experienced a lot of human pathology and dis-ease arising from the fear or experience of three things: rejection, abandonment, and failure. However, being rooted in our God-given identity can help us heal and overcome any related setbacks or trauma stemming from these experiences.

Mark's Gospel notes that during Jesus' baptism, God speaks directly to Jesus and says, "You are my beloved son; with you I am well pleased." Understand that God affirmed Jesus in love ("my beloved"), in relationship and position ("son" – which spoke to divine connection and position of authority), and in acceptance ("I am well pleased with you"). God's affirmation of His identity as Beloved Son would be just the preparation and protection that Jesus would need as He would next face The Adversary in the wilderness, and then a ministry where He would experience rejection and being misunderstood.

DATE / /

Day 5

(Thursday): Resting in Your God-Given Identity

Thought for Today

In the same way, as sons and daughters of God, walking faithfully in the ways of Jesus, we too can be assured that God loves us, that we have a place with God, we are accepted by God, and God takes pleasure in us. That is both preparation for times when we don't have a big fan club, and we are misunderstood; and protection from the fiery darts of the enemy that would try to make us behave ourselves in ways that conflict with our identity as mature sons and daughters of God and derail us from our mission. We can rest from the often toxic and destructive ways we demonstrate the need to fight narratives spun out of other people's opinions and prove ourselves to those around us that we are worthy of love.

Friend, in Christ, you are a beloved Son or Daughter of God, in whom God is well-pleased. Rest in that. Be rooted in that. Be healed in that. Soar in that.

MY REFLECTIONS

DATE / /

Day 6

(Friday): Who is your T.E.A.M.?

Thought for Today

"for they refreshed my spirit as well as yours. Give recognition to such people."
(1 Corinthians 16:18, ESV)

Part of self-care and living in wholeness includes having and nurturing healthy relationships that nourish our spirits. A God-given network of mutual exchange for purpose and destiny.

It is important for us, especially at crucial moments in our lives, to take stock of those around us and understand their place in our lives and embrace the comfort and discomfort that they bring that will propel and even provoke us into our purpose and vice-versa.

So, allow me to share with you a helpful acronym, T.E.A.M., that represent the types of people that we should ask God to send into our lives:

DATE / /

Day 6

(Friday): Who is your T.E.A.M.?

Thought for Today

T – Truth-Tellers

These are the people who will consistently tell you the unadulterated truth – not what you want to hear, but what you need to hear. No one needs to be surrounded by "yes" people, and as Jesus said, it is the truth that makes us free.

E – Endurers

Yes, "endurers" is a completely made-up word, but I trust that you'll get it. "Endurers" are those who are loyal and committed to us for love's sake – capable of loving us to our best, and at and through our worst.

A – Accountability Figures

These are the people who help us set and maintain healthy boundaries in our lives. They can be friends, but they can also be people like pastors, financial managers, therapists, fitness trainers, and coaches.

M – Mentors and Mentees

We all need someone who is pouring into us for our advancement in a particular area of our lives, and we need to be doing the same for others.

So, who is your T.E.A.M.? Are there areas where people are missing? If so, make it a point to strategically seek God about bringing the right people onto your T.E.A.M. and being able to discern them when they show up.

MY REFLECTIONS

DAY: 7 (Saturday)

SELF-CARE IN ACTION

Make Time for Your T.E.A.M.

When is the last time that you intentionally made time for those that add value to your life? It's easy to get "lost in the sauce" of life and neglect the nurturing of important relationships. When's the last time you had a day of enjoyment with your bestie or friend group? Maybe it's time to check in with your mentor or mentee, or have an accountability session concerning your finances, ministry, or mental health. Do you sense that your T.E.A.M. needs to grow or even shift in one or more areas? Below make your plan about how you will engage with or even grow your T.E.A.M. in the near future.

DAY: 7 (Saturday)

SELF-CARE IN ACTION

Make Time for Your T.E.A.M.

Who on my T.E.A.M. do I need to make time with right now? What are my plans to connect with them and when?

____

____

____

____

____

____

Is the Holy Spirit signaling me that my T.E.A.M. needs to grow or even shift in one or more areas? If so, how?

____

____

____

____

____

____

DAY: 8 (Sunday)
DISCOVERY AND CARE PLANNING DAY

What have you discovered about God this week? What have you discovered about yourself this week?

____

____

____

____

____

____

How I plan to experience rest and engage in self-care this week?

____

____

____

____

____

____

DATE / /

Day 9

(Monday): Resting in God's Provision

Thought for Today

"You gave your good Spirit to instruct them and did not withhold your manna from their mouth and gave them water for their thirst."
(Nehemiah 9:20, ESV)

How one is going to survive and thrive is often a major source of stress and ambition for many people. However, one of the refrains that we see throughout Scripture is the challenge to trust God as our ultimate Source of all things that are good and necessary for life.

In recalling the Israelites' experience in the wilderness, by all external evidence, they had every reason to be concerned about how they were going to survive. While slaves in Egypt they could count on their "leeks and onions," (Numbers 11:4-6) but now, although free from slavery and Pharaoh's rule, they were in the middle of a wilderness without food or water in sight, brought there by the God of their ancestors. As the narrative goes, God provided an unknown substance for them from heaven each day called manna. They were told they would receive enough for each day, and twice the amount the day before Sabbath, so they could properly honor the Sabbath on the seventh day. God faithfully provided manna every day without fail for them for forty years.

DATE / /

Day 9

(Monday): Resting in God's Provision

Thought for Today

It is interesting that there is a question built into the etymology of the word manna, for it means in Hebrew, "What is it?" I believe this teaches us that we must be comfortable with the mystery of God's provision. Meaning there will always have to be an element of trust that what God gives is good for us, how much God gives is enough for what we need, and that how God decides to get that provision to us is a matter of God's sovereignty and that we should not allow it to be a source of worry for us.

If worry about provision (wisdom, money, other resources, etc.) has been a challenge in your life, I encourage you to: first release any tendency to want to control all outcomes, second, rest in the goodness and wisdom of God who delights in being your Source; third, don't be afraid to seek help when you've exhausted your strategies. God often uses people to graciously provide. You never know whom God has prepared to assist you if you ask.

MY REFLECTIONS

DATE / /

Day 10

(Tuesday): I Can't Love You If I Don't Love Me

Thought for Today

God-centered self-care is not an exercise in narcissism or self-centeredness, but a call for us to understand the seriousness of Jesus's words in Matthew 11:28.

There Jesus said that the two greatest commandments that fulfill all the rest are to love God, and to love your neighbor as yourself.

We often gloss over those last two powerful words – as yourself-- or we, in a very surface way, tend to interpret it as another articulation of The Golden Rule.

However, "…as yourself" brings self-care sharply into view. What if we understood the second commandment to mean that we can only love our neighbors to the extent that we love ourselves! Therefore, if we don't know or practice what it means to love ourselves, we cannot fully live out Jesus's call to love our neighbor.

DATE / /

Day 10

(Tuesday): I Can't Love You If I Don't Love Me

Thought for Today

Loving ourselves often involves learning languages and practices that lend themselves towards wholeness while un-learning the ones that don't. It also involves bringing some of the people around us or new people we encounter closer in while being okay with releasing others. Above all, loving ourselves begins with seeing ourselves the way God sees us, as God's wonderfully made creation (see Psalm 139:14)!

So now, think of and write down 3 things that affirm how wonderful God has made you. Try to include at least one thing that is not achievement-based. Then, take a moment to internalize the fact that these wonderful things about you are a gift from God, and give God thanks! In moments when you are not feeling your best, come back to these 3 things to give you encouragement and strength.

MY REFLECTIONS

DAY: **11 (Wednesday)**
SELF-CARE CHECK-IN DAY

Self-Care Listening: How am I feeling today?

Are my body, mind/emotions giving me any signals that I need to slow down and pay attention to today?

DAY: 11 (Wednesday)
SELF-CARE CHECK-IN DAY

How can I partner with God to give myself or receive the support I need?

How do I need to let others know how they can support me today?

DATE / /

Day 12

(Thursday): Forgiveness, Pt. 1: Forgiving Others

Thought for Today

If we look at the word forgive, we see for-give. But who is the gift for? Primarily, forgiveness is a gift that we give ourselves. The gift of being free to live a life not trapped and bound by bitterness and the memories surrounding pain and trauma. It is a gift that allows us the space to heal and become whole.

When instructing His disciples, Jesus told them (and us who choose to be His disciples today) to forgive others as a part of our daily conversation with God (see Luke 11:4). Why is forgiveness a part of prayer? Because forgiveness is not a feeling, rather, it has everything to do with power, and our view and use of power should be informed by daily conversations with God. Forgiveness deals with the power and free agency that we have to decide what we will do about the offense and the offender. Will we relinquish our power to live in wholeness, waiting on an apology from the offender?

DATE / /

Day 12

(Thursday): Forgiveness, Pt. 1: Forgiving Others

Thought for Today

Will we place ourselves in the place of God as judge and jury by remaining in bitterness or by exacting revenge, or will we willingly entrust the process and power of justice to God and God's sovereign wisdom? Do we trust that God is big enough to shepherd us through the process of healing from wounds without having to hold on to them?

Certainly, forgiveness does not mean that the offender is free of the consequences (natural or spiritual) of his/her actions, nor does it mean that reconciliation with the offender will take place, as reconciliation requires that the offender completely take ownership of his/her actions, take the necessary steps to regain trust that they will not re-offend, and do what is needed to bring about restitution for the original offense. If these prerequisites are not met, then reconciliation is not possible – nor is it required. However, the good news is, is that we don't have to wait for an apology to forgive. We are empowered to move forward with our lives and undertake our journey of healing without an apology or acknowledgement from the offender, trusting that The One is whose hands is all power, is able to navigate us through every peak and valley towards wholeness.

MY REFLECTIONS

DATE / /

Day 13

(Friday): Forgiveness, part 2: Forgiving Ourselves

Thought for Today

For some of us, releasing resentment towards others is not currently an issue, but some of us may need to forgive ourselves for our poor, unwise, or uninformed decisions, even those that have actively and deeply caused harm to others. Regret, guilt, and shame can turn into poisons and prisons that keep us from moving forward. Unforgiveness towards the self limits us to a singular moment in time and does not allow us the space or opportunity for true growth and transformation, or to be released into the wholeness that God intends for us all.

Although we understand that forgiveness does not mean being free of the consequences of our actions (or inaction), it is also not God's desire that we continue to hold ourselves hostage to the mistakes we've made, especially if we have taken steps to learn from them and make things right. Scripture is full of examples of broken people that caused brokenness to themselves, their families, and their communities (think David and Paul). But their stories do not end there – they experience the forgiveness and grace of God that does not limit them to that singular moment, but allows them to grow, evolve, and even become agents of transformation themselves. With God's grace, we must allow ourselves that same opportunity.

DATE / /

Day 13

(Friday): Forgiveness, part 2: Forgiving Ourselves

Thought for Today

Forgiving ourselves begins with taking accountability for our decisions and actions. Sometimes we make unwise or poor choices because we didn't know better. Truth is, we don't know what we don't know, but when we know, we are responsible for doing better. And then, some of us did know better – we acted out of fear, our own selfish desires, or out of being hurt ourselves. Whatever the circumstance, let's consider some things that will help us embrace forgiving ourselves:

1. Know and understand that God operates out of a place of love for you. Embracing that you are deeply loved by God will help center your perspective that you are worth loving and will be a reminder that you can forgive yourself.

2. With the understanding that you cannot change the past, be honest about what occurred, and take accountability for your role, and for what you can do moving forward. Although it may be difficult do, repent (meaning: do differently) to God and to anyone that you are aware of that you've hurt.

DATE / /

Day 13

(Friday): Forgiveness, part 2: Forgiving Ourselves

Thought for Today

Remember, we can't bypass the people we've hurt and claim that because we've "asked God for forgiveness" that that suffices. Jesus admonishes us in Matthew 5:23-24 that if we come before God and we are aware that we have offended someone, we are to leave our gift for God at the altar and go be reconciled with the person we have potentially offended.

3. While a sincere apology goes a long way, more is often required to bring wholeness. Do what you can to mend broken relationships and make right what you did wrong. Understand that people you have hurt may not be (or ever be) ready to forgive or receive you but do your part to sincerely ask for their forgiveness and make appropriate restitution.

4. Decide daily to release any feelings of guilt, shame, regret, and unworthiness. Left to linger and fester, these emotions can lead to anxiety, depression, and even physical conditions.

Remember, God's ultimate intent for you is to live in wholeness and that includes being in wholeness with yourself.

MY REFLECTIONS

DAY:14 (Saturday)

SELF-CARE IN ACTION

Developing Healthy Habits Around Sleep

"In peace I will both lie down and sleep, for you alone, O LORD, make me dwell in safety."
(Psalm 4:8, ESV)

Adequate sleep is, of course, key for a healthy body and mind, and your age and level of activity are factors in the amount of sleep that you need each night. However, it's not only about the number of hours that you sleep, but that you have created an optimal environment holistically for your body and mind to repair itself during sleep. It is during this nightly healing process that your body and mind are at rest, and you can even receive clarity, insight, and answers from God.

If you are having difficulty achieving restful sleep, it could be due to a number of factors (stress, underlying health issues, etc.), but developing a sleep routine can be helpful. Here are a few tips to help you get started, but feel free to add things that work for you:

DAY: **14 (Saturday)**

SELF-CARE IN ACTION

Developing Healthy Habits Around Sleep

1. Try taking at least 30 minutes before going to bed to pray and release the pressures of the day. Do your best to avoid stressful/heavy conversations before bed, and meditate on Scripture, the goodness of God, and what you are grateful for.

2. Be mindful of the programming you watch and/or listen to before bed as they do affect your consciousness.

3. Have an unplugged quiet time before bed: disconnect from emails, phone calls, and social media.

4. Do your best to ensure your sleeping environment is dark, comfortable temperature, and quiet.

5. Avoid caffeine and heavy meals in the hours before bed.

Are there any other things you can think of that you would like to implement as part of your sleep routine?

MY REFLECTIONS

DAY :15 (Sunday)
DISCOVERY AND CARE PLANNING DAY

What have you discovered about God this week? What have you discovered about yourself this week?

____

____

____

____

____

____

How I plan to experience rest and engage in self-care this week?

____

____

____

____

____

____

DATE / /

Day 16

(Monday): Boundaries Part 1: Capacity

Thought for Today

One of the hallmarks of self-care is setting and enforcing proper boundaries around the resources of our time, attention, energy, and tangible resources. Boundaries are important because they are a way to honestly communicate our capacity in an area at a given season of our lives, and they are the marks of good stewardship (management).

The key to boundaries is balance, for an abundant life is a balanced life where every area of your life is attended to and thriving. A balanced life is certainly a journey with ebbs and flows, but it is something we should be striving towards, and acknowledging our capacity is a part of that.

Take some time today and reflect on your capacity. The questions below are designed to help you as you reflect.

DATE / /

Day 16

(Monday): Boundaries Part 1: Capacity

Thought for Today

- What areas of your life feel balanced (i.e., physical, or spiritual health, friendships, career)?

o It's important to name and celebrate where we are thriving, and even note the strategies that we employ in our thriving areas as they may provide insight on how to bring balance into other areas.

- Where do you have room to give?

o Are you in a space in your life where perhaps you have extra time or other resources (extra meaning, after you have met your deliverables, including caring for yourself)? How might God be calling you to meaningfully use this extra time or these resources?

- In what areas are you feeling overextended in your capacity?

o What actions can you take immediately to bring your capacity into balance?

o Have you communicated with others in your life your need to bring balance into an area, and that you may need their assistance in doing so?

o What can you delegate to others so that you can experience greater balance?

MY REFLECTIONS

DATE / /

Day 17

(Tuesday): Boundaries, Part 2: Time...

Seize the Day!

Thought for Today

"So, teach us to consider our mortality so that we might live wisely."
(Psalm 90:12, NET)

As much as we perhaps would like to believe that we have all the time in the world, Psalm 90 (and Ecclesiastes, for that matter), and life experiences provide us with glaring reminders that our time on earth is fleeting, and in view of that, we ought to live wisely. Living wisely includes how we steward our resources: the resources of our bodies, minds, gifts, money, time, and more. While I'm sure we can all think of plenty of things to remind us that life is fleeting and serious, living wisely also means making the most of our days, which includes not only completing "work" tasks, but spending time with those we hold dear, and not putting off purposeful plans that give our lives meaning, as well as plans for leisure and enjoyment.

In thinking about living life meaningfully, here are some reflections to consider:

When is the last time that you prioritized quality time with your loved ones, and being fully present with them in that moment?

DATE / /

Day 17

(Tuesday): Boundaries, Part 2: Time...

Seize the Day!

Thought for Today

When is the last time that you made time to do something enjoyable just for you?

Is there anything in your life that you would like to accomplish that you have allowed to sit on the backburner? What will it take to prioritize that goal? It may be that you simply need to give yourself permission to proceed!

These are all reflections that, if we answer them honestly and prioritize following through on them help us to live our lives wisely and meaningfully in light of the fact that we will not be on earth forever.

Can you think of any other areas of your life that need prioritization right now?

MY REFLECTIONS

DAY: 18 (Wednesday)
SELF-CARE CHECK-IN DAY

Self-Care Listening: How am I feeling today?

Are my body, mind/emotions giving me any signals that I need to slow down and pay attention to today?

DAY: 18 (Wednesday)
SELF-CARE CHECK-IN DAY

How can I partner with God to give myself or receive the support I need?

How do I need to let others know how they can support me today?

DATE / /

Day 19

(Thursday): Boundaries Part 3: Space

Thought for Today

Over the past decade or so "man-caves" and "she-sheds" have become very popular. People have transformed their basements, spare bedrooms, or even portable tiny sheds into places of respite and solace.

This trend strikes an important chord in the human experience: that everyone needs a place of their own to pray, meditate, reflect, journal, be creative, or just…breathe. Even Jesus consistently found a quiet place to be alone.

While your living conditions may or may not allow you a defined space just to yourself, what matters is finding/defining a quiet place somewhere that ministers to you and brings you peace. It might be a park, a room (or corner of a room) in your home, or a chapel that is open to the public to sit quietly and/or pray.

Do you have a favorite place for quiet time? If so, what about it draws you to it and brings you peace? If not, can you think of some places (either at home or somewhere else) that might be a good fit for a quiet place for you? Go on a quest and explore some of those places this week that might meet your quiet time needs.

MY REFLECTIONS

DATE / /

Day 20

(Friday): Boundaries, pt 4: Power of "No"

Thought for Today

"Now the Jewish Feast of Shelters was near. 3 So Jesus' brothers advised him, "Leave here and go to Judea so your disciples may see your miracles that you are performing. 4 For no one who seeks to make a reputation for himself does anything in secret. If you are doing these things, show yourself to the world." 5 (For not even his own brothers believed in him.) 6 So Jesus replied, "My time has not yet arrived, but you are ready at any opportunity! 7 The world cannot hate you, but it hates me, because I am testifying about it that its deeds are evil. 8 You go up to the feast yourselves. I am not going up to this feast because my time has not yet fully arrived."

(John 7:2-8, NET)

Do you, or have you ever had an issue with telling others "no," even to the detriment of yourself? Sometimes, even with the best of intentions, we overextend ourselves: our time, energy, even money and other tangible resources. There are a number of reasons that can lead us to overextend: a tendency towards "people-pleasing" and wanting to be accepted, fear of rejection if we say no, unhealthy ambition, or some other underlying fear. Some of us feel if we say no it means that we are not capable or have failed in some way.

DATE / /

Day 20

(Friday): Boundaries, pt 4: Power of "No"

Thought for Today

No matter the reason, overextending ourselves often leads to burnout, mental and emotional angst, financial strain, damage to personal and professional relationships, and so much more. So, it is important that we learn how to set and honor boundaries that preserve and sustain our wellbeing, learning when to say "no" is a part of that.

One of the things that I admire most about Jesus was His firm sense of self (identity and mission) which enabled Him to unapologetically say no when necessary. He said no to unnecessary conversations, debates, tasks, and even doing good deeds that did not align with who He was and what He was sent to do. He said no to the unnecessary so that He could have time and energy for the necessary.

Knowing when to say no is not so much about who you are not, but knowing and honoring who you are, and where your time, energy, and resources are best spent in that moment, and having the confidence to communicate that to others even when they don't understand or agree.

DATE / /

Day 20

(Friday): Boundaries, pt 4: Power of “No”

Thought for Today

It may take time and/or practice to become comfortable with setting and enforcing your boundaries, but remember, it is an act of love towards yourself, that will ultimately lead to you being the best you for yourself and others.

MY REFLECTIONS

DAY: 21 (Saturday)

SELF-CARE IN ACTION

Plan a Spa Day!

When is the last time that you pampered yourself? Gotten a massage, a mani/pedi, or taken a trip to an actual spa? Well, it's time to plan one! You can even have a spa day at home or with friends! The key is to set aside time to engage the body in relaxation and wellness. Now remember, accountability is a part of self-care, so be sure to set an actual day and time (at least 4 hours, but one entire day would be optimal) to have your spa day. I encourage you to make spa-day a part of your regular self-care routine. Use the space below to help you plan your next spa day, or spa day routine.

My Spa Day

Where: ____

What I will do (trip to a day spa, mani/pedi, massage, etc.)

____

____

With Whom (alone, with spouse or friends):

____

____

When (Date and Time): ______________________________

MY REFLECTIONS

DAY :22 (Sunday)
DISCOVERY AND CARE PLANNING DAY

What have you discovered about God this week? What have you discovered about yourself this week?

____

____

____

____

____

____

How I plan to experience rest and engage in self-care this week?

____

____

____

____

____

____

DATE / /

Day 23

(Monday): Stewardship of Our Bodies

Thought for Today

Or do you not know that your body is the temple of the Holy Spirit who is in you, whom you have from God, and you are not your own? 20 For you were bought at a price. Therefore, glorify God with your body.
(1 Corinthians 6:19-20, NET)

The creation accounts in Genesis 1-2 tell us that while God created most of the world by speaking, when it came to humanity, God took a more personal approach and formed a human body from the dust of the ground. No one takes that kind of time and care into forming something with their own hands that is not valuable and important. Our bodies, no matter their size, shape, color, or states of ableness are a gift from God to help us sense, navigate, appreciate, and enjoy the world around us, and to glorify God. Think about that: God is glorified with our bodies, and the Holy Spirit values our bodies so much that the Spirit chooses to dwell there, and Paul calls it a temple (a sacred space)! And part of our response to God's grace is to care for (steward) the temple that Holy Spirit indwells, for we bear witness to God's grace not only with how we use our bodies, but how we care for our bodies.

DATE / /

Day 23

(Monday): Stewardship of Our Bodies

Thought for Today

Abuse of or lack of stewardship over our physical bodies can take on many forms: the ones that typically come to mind are abuse of alcohol, drugs, smoking, and self-harm, but over- and/or under-eating, the abuse of sex, and lack of proper rest also reflect improper stewardship of our bodies. Scripture tells us that ultimately our bodies were made to glorify God, so what practices can we employ to glorify God in caring for our bodies? Here are a few:

1. Listen to your body. If you begin to experience unusual signals/symptoms in your body, don't ignore them -- address them as soon as you can. Learn when your body needs movement and when it needs to rest.
2. Fuel your body – put things in your body that are nutritious and help your body function at its best, and at times our bodies require different things. And, of course, it's okay to indulge every now and then, but do your best to exercise moderation on a daily basis. Just like you wouldn't put sugar in your gas tank, don't live to eat, but eat to live.

DATE / /

Day 23

(Monday): Stewardship of Our Bodies

Thought for Today

3. Rest your body. The human body needs adequate rest to function properly. Discover and develop healthy habits around sleep.

4. Appreciate your body. Our bodies come in all shapes, sizes, and states of ableness. God does not want our bodies to be sources of shame, guilt, or loathing, whether our bodies appear or function the way we desire them to or not. Remember, our bodies were made to glorify God, not us.

How is your current stewardship of your body bringing glory to God?

MY REFLECTIONS

DATE / /

Day 24

(Tuesday): It's Time to Declutter!

Thought for Today

"He sets the time for finding and the time for losing, the time for saving and the time for throwing away."

(Ecclesiastes 3:6, Good News Translation)

Ah, yes, decluttering: a word that excites some, and incites dread in others. But no matter where you fall on the spectrum of "decluttering enjoyability," it's something that we all must do regularly, and while we could certainly focus on the benefits of removing unnecessary clutter from our physical spaces, what strategies do you currently have in place to mentally and emotionally declutter?

Setting aside time daily to release the experiences of the day before God, process them through the lens of the Holy Spirit, and recenter is important. Why daily? Well, let's think about our physical homes: what happens when we allow dirty dishes, laundry, unnecessary items, and the other signs of daily living to accumulate day after day without putting them in their proper place? We look up and find that we have a big mess on our hands that takes more effort to clean up than if we had set a bit of time aside daily to deal with it.

DATE / /

Day 24

(Tuesday): It's Time to Declutter!

Thought for Today

Some of us may pride ourselves on keeping a spotless home, but our interior life has not been attended to in ages. We are carrying years of disappointment, frustration, stress, anxiety, and perhaps even trauma, and have allowed them to pile up inside. Eventually, like our physical homes, our souls run out of space to hold those experiences, and what we are holding begins to show up in our lives in ways we (and those around us) probably never expected such as in our mental and physical health, and the way we engage with others daily.

What I find interesting about the above translation of Ecclesiastes 3:6 is that it highlights that it is **God** who sets the time for saving things and for releasing them! This means that God knows not only **what** needs to be released, but also **when**. This is why setting time aside to be alone with ourselves and God daily is important. Communing with God and sitting quietly with ourselves each day makes space for us to tend to our spiritual, emotional, and mental build ups, and makes us more sensitive to internal issues that may require more specialized time, attention, and strategy to tend to.

DATE / /

Day 24

(Tuesday): It's Time to Declutter!

Thought for Today

Here are a few tips to practice daily mental and emotional decluttering:

1. If you don't currently have quiet time set aside each day for you and God, commit to setting some aside – even if it's in smaller chunks throughout the day (10 minutes in the morning, 10 during lunch, 10 before bed), just start somewhere, and be sure that it is in a space where you can be free of distraction.

2. Quiet your mind. I know that this can be a challenge initially, but don't get frustrated – employ the discipline of focus to assist you. Be patient with yourself. Focus your mind on something you are grateful to God for in that moment, or a Scripture that currently resonates with you.

3. Breathe deeply, and in light of your focus points, release before God anything that needs tending to in your soul, or even that you need clarity or strategy about. If you need to lament or laugh, do so. Be confident in knowing that you can trust God with whatever you've released.

Thought for Today

4. Sit in quiet expectation and allow space for the Holy Spirit to minister to you, or just sit quietly in silence. You may sense an impression, a Scripture, a song, a word, or experience silence. If silence is uncomfortable for you, don't get discouraged: silence is not the absence of action, it is often God creating space for the next meaningful step to take place. Any and all of these ways that God ministers to us help us keep our mental and emotional space free and can provide us with perspective that we need for processing our experiences.

5. If you feel led and find it helpful, journal what you experience, and be open throughout the day (or the following day) to how you may experience God's power and presence.

MY REFLECTIONS

DAY: **25 (Wednesday)**
SELF-CARE CHECK-IN DAY

Self-Care Listening: How am I feeling today?

____

____

____

____

____

____

____

Are my body, mind/emotions giving me any signals that I need to slow down and pay attention to today?

____

____

____

____

____

____

DAY: 25 (Wednesday)
SELF-CARE CHECK-IN DAY

How can I partner with God to give myself or receive the support I need?

How do I need to let others know how they can support me today?

DATE / /

Day 26

(Thursday): Good Grief

Thought for Today

For everything there is an appointed time, and an appropriate time for every activity on earth…a time to weep, and a time to laugh; a time to mourn, and a time to dance.

Ecclesiastes 3:1,4 (NET)

Grieving? As self-care? Yes, when done in a healthy manner. Loss, whether it is the loss of a loved one, a marriage to divorce, a job, or something else, is a part of our journey through this life, and so it is necessary to obtain and develop the tools and skills necessary to care for ourselves while navigating these difficult moments.

We must first understand that there is nothing wrong with grieving. In fact, the writer of Ecclesiastes tells us that there is indeed a time to mourn; meaning that we must take time to acknowledge that a loss has occurred and begin the process of orienting ourselves to a life that looks different after that loss. What that time of grieving looks like and how long it lasts for each person is different. Depending on the type of loss, such as the loss of a loved one, we may never "get over it," but instead, with God's help and time, we find ways to move forward in life-giving and life-affirming ways.

DATE / /

Day 26

(Thursday): Good Grief

Thought for Today

Burying our emotions (or allowing them to consume us), trying to rush ourselves through the grieving process, or allowing others to push us into "moving on" do not support healthy grieving.

Here are a few considerations for grieving in a healthy way:

1. Acknowledge that a loss has occurred, whether it was yesterday, or something that happened years ago that has gone unaddressed. Be honest about how that has affected/is affecting you.
2. Be kind to yourself and take small steps. Take the time and space you need to process the loss, and don't allow others' discomfort with your grief cause you to rush your healing journey.
3. Be clear and open about your boundaries surrounding your loss and require that others honor them. You don't have to engage in conversations or activities that you are not yet ready for as you are healing and navigating your process.
4. If you find that the loss is interfering with your quality of life, in addition to engaging your spiritual habits (like prayer), seek the aid of a counselor/therapist who can help you talk and work through your grief in healthy ways.

MY REFLECTIONS

DATE / /

Day 27

(Friday): Loving God with Your Mind: Embracing Your Creativity

Thought for Today

And you shall love the Lord your God with all your heart and with all your soul and with all your mind and with all your strength.

(Mark 12:30, ESV)

When is the last time you created something? If we look at the world around us, we can see divine creativity on display. Have you ever taken the time to consider all of the species of birds, animals, trees, and flowers there are, and really allowed it soak in that all that we see in this world is the result of the creativity of God? And note, that while everything had purpose, the creation account in Genesis is careful to tell us that God also created things that were aesthetically pleasing (Genesis 2:9). If then, we are created in God's image, part of that means that we, too, should be engaging our creative side -- creating not just for utility, but also for beauty and our enjoyment!

When we use the minds God gave us to create something to uplift, inspire, elevate humanity, and draw people to God, we are loving God with our minds. Today you are encouraged to embrace your creativity as a divine expression.

MY REFLECTIONS

DAY: 28 (Saturday)
SELF-CARE IN ACTION

What is your favorite area of creative expression? Writing or performing music, short stories, or poetry? Cooking? Baking? Dance? Graphic design? Theater? Knitting? Painting? Pottery? There are endless possibilities…

DAY :28 (Saturday)
SELF-CARE IN ACTION

When is the last time that you engaged your creative side not related to your job or business, or that was not task-related? Or maybe there is an area of creativity that you've always wanted to try, but never made time to do it. Now is the time to just that. You never know what you'll discover about yourself in the process!

DAY: 28 (Saturday)
SELF-CARE IN ACTION

Take some time this week to get in touch with your creative side and pick up your favorite area of creativity that you haven't engaged in a while, or a new one that you'd like to try.

DAY :29 (Sunday)
DISCOVERY AND CARE PLANNING DAY

What have you discovered about God this week? What have you discovered about yourself this week?

How I plan to experience rest and engage in self-care this week?

DATE / /

Day 30

(Monday): Be Kind to Yourself - Silencing Negative Self-Talk

Thought for Today

My grandmother used to say, "It's a poor frog that doesn't praise its own pond!" In other words, you shouldn't be afraid or ashamed to speak well about yourself. Today let's go into a bit of a deeper dive into our previous encouragement to love ourselves (see Day 10). Part of loving yourself includes taking an honest look at how you speak about and to yourself. What are the internal conversations that you are having each day? Are you finding more fault with yourself than extending yourself the grace to grow? Do you overly-criticize yourself when you don't meet an expectation? Or perhaps you downplay yourself in groups because you have hidden insecurities. After some reflection, if you find that you speak down to yourself more often than not, it's time to reprogram your internal conversations, which reflect your core beliefs about yourself. You may need to enlist the assistance of a counselor or therapist to help you with this process of uncovering and healing from more deeply-rooted self-talk rooted in pain, trauma, and other negative experiences.

DATE / /

Day 30

(Monday): Be Kind to Yourself - Silencing Negative Self-Talk

Thought for Today

Then, anchor yourself in what God says about you. Psalm 139:14 (NRSVUE) declares: “I praise you, for I am fearfully and wonderfully made. Wonderful are your works; that I know very well.” How well have you embraced that you are indeed a wonderful work of God? Embracing that knowing begins with telling yourself that, especially in the moments when you don’t feel like a wonderful work of God and allowing that declaration to be a comfort and a standard by which you live and love yourself.

Remember, wholeness is a journey, and it begins with honesty, a willingness to confront and address difficult things, and by learning and embracing how God sees you.

MY REFLECTIONS

DATE / /

Day 31

(Tuesday): Silence is Golden

Thought for Today

Like apples of gold in settings of silver, so is a word skillfully spoken.
(Proverbs 25:11, NET)

Have you ever participated in a silent retreat, or intentionally engaged in a set time of silence? Did you notice that despite how challenging it may have been to keep silent at the beginning by the end of that set time you were much more thoughtful about your words moving forward?

The world itself was created by divine speech, and the writers of Scripture from Proverbs to James admonish us about how powerful speech is. Even the book of Revelation describes the heavenly realm engaging in a time of silence for a time (Revelation 8:1).

Taking a set time to refrain from speaking is a way for us to engage in a meaningful pause to reset, listen, reflect on the ways that we can use our words more meaningfully and skillfully. Silence also helps identify areas of healing that need to take place in our lives: are we one that is uncomfortable with silence? Do we always have to fill in quiet gaps with speech?

DATE / /

Day 31

(Tuesday): Silence is Golden

Thought for Today

If so, we should probably explore where our discomfort with silence comes from. Is it an expression of social anxiety, or is it ultimately a sign of discomfort with ourselves in some way?

Whatever the case, intentional moments or times of silence helps us build the discipline of knowing what to say, when to say it, and even how to say it. If you have never taken intentional times to engage in silence, prayerfully take some time to do so. Ask God during this time to show you ways that your words can be used more meaningfully and skillfully to build up, encourage, create, and effect change in your life and the environments around you.

MY REFLECTIONS

DAY: 32 (Wednesday)
SELF-CARE CHECK-IN DAY

Self-Care Listening: How am I feeling today?

Are my body, mind/emotions giving me any signals that I need to slow down and pay attention to today?

DAY: 32 (Wednesday)
SELF-CARE CHECK-IN DAY

How can I partner with God to give myself or receive the support I need?

How do I need to let others know how they can support me today?

DATE / /

Day 33

(Thursday): A Meaningful Pause: "Come Away and Rest Awhile"

Thought for Today

"The apostles returned to Jesus and told him all that they had done and taught. And he said to them, "Come away by yourselves to a desolate place and rest a while."

(Mark 6:30-31, ESV)

Imagine the excitement of the apostles after returning to Jesus and sharing their ministry experiences on the road – all that they had seen, heard, and experienced! Demons cast out, bodies healed, hearts turned towards God – they had the opportunity to put into practice the things they had learned from Jesus, not only from His teaching, but also from His demonstration.

But Jesus' response is not to hurry them on to the next task, but He invites them into four key things:

1. Come away: they are invited to a change of scenery
2. To a desolate [literally desert] place: they are invited to a place of simplicity and free from distractions
3. Rest/Refresh yourselves: they are invited to rest and recharge to prepare them for whatever would come next

Day 33

(Thursday): A Meaningful Pause: "Come Away and Rest Awhile"

Thought for Today

4. For a while: the exact amount of time for rest was not dictated, allowing them the freedom to prioritize rest without worrying about time constraints.

These four key parts of Jesus' charge to the disciples serve as key ingredients for times of refreshing for us, particularly after a significant moment or major accomplishment in our lives. It is important that we resist the temptation to ride high on the wave of success into the next thing without taking the time to process, reflect, and recharge for whatever lies just ahead.

As busy people, we often prioritize the needs of everyone else, and at times feel a sense of guilt prioritizing our own needs, but today Holy Spirit bids us to take appropriate times to pause and rest for our next.

Have you been sensing the need the "Come away…and rest awhile"? Have you noticed any signals in your body and emotions indicating that it is time to do so? If you are in a place where you are rested and recharged, what are the typical signals in your body and emotional state that help you know it's time to rest?

MY REFLECTIONS

DATE / /

Day 34

(Friday): "Back to Life, Back to Reality"

Thought for Today

"In these days he went out to the mountain to pray, and all night he continued in prayer to God. And when day came, he called his disciples and chose from them twelve, whom he named apostles…"
(Luke 6:12-13, NET)

Yesterday we explored the importance of pulling away for a meaningful pause. Today, let's explore how to reengage in the rhythm of life afterwards.

In Luke 6, Jesus spends all night in prayer alone with God, and out of that time of spiritual connection and renewal, He comes back to reengage with those around Him in fruitful ways. He emerges with clarity and vision that gives definition to his community, and He emerges with supernatural power and grace that provides wholeness to others.

But, if we're honest, reengaging after a time of rest is not always easy, as jumping back into the swing of things can sometimes be jarring to our bodies and emotions. For instance, maybe you (and your family) have had some vacation time and now it's time to get back into the swing of things at home, work, school, church, etc.

DATE / /

Day 34

(Friday): "Back to Life, Back to Reality"

Thought for Today

So, how can we minimize some of the pressure points of reengaging with the rhythm of our everyday routine so that our reengagement is fruitful and beneficial beyond the moment to us and those around us? Here are a few suggestions:

1. Before reengaging, make note of what you have gained from your time away. What clarity, new perspectives or solutions have you gained? How have you changed? What's different now if anything? What do you realize that you need now that you didn't before? Journaling can help you process your insights.

2. If at all possible, take at least one day between your time away, and your return back to work/home life/normalcy to readjust. Only prioritize action items that are pressing. Resist the urge to rush into anything too heavy and give yourself a moment to readjust to your normal environment. Pay attention to your body signals and how you're feeling as you reengage.

Day 34

(Friday): "Back to Life, Back to Reality"

Thought for Today

3. Give yourself and those around you grace. If you're not quite "back" yet, it's okay. Communicate honestly with others as you're readjusting about where you are physically and mentally as you engage with them. Especially if you spent time away alone, understand that your community around you is readjusting to your presence as well. Take some deep breaths and, as people say, "keep it light."

MY REFLECTIONS

DAY: **35 (Saturday)**

SELF-CARE IN ACTION

Unplugged

In thinking about Jesus' invitation to "Come away and rest awhile," here are some suggestions for removing distractions and embracing a change of scenery:

1. Go for a scenic drive, bike ride, or walk.
2. Commit to at least one phone/device-free meal each day, and instead engage with your family or music you enjoy instead.
3. Make use of your phone/device's "do not disturb/focus/mute" features to enhance quiet times you've set aside.
4. Plan a staycation or short getaway just for yourself.

Maybe you already have a solid strategy for physical and mental respite when needed, but what about your spiritual life? Is there anything occupying your time that may be leading to a disconnect in your walk with God/spiritual disciplines?

MY REFLECTIONS

DAY: 36 (Sunday)

DISCOVERY AND CARE PLANNING DAY

What have you discovered about God this week? What have you discovered about yourself this week?

____

____

____

____

____

____

How I plan to experience rest and engage in self-care this week?

____

____

____

____

____

____

MY REFLECTIONS

DAY: **37 (Monday)**
SELF-CARE CHECK-IN DAY

Self-Care Listening: How am I feeling today?

Are my body, mind/emotions giving me any signals that I need to slow down and pay attention to today?

DAY: **37 (Monday)**
SELF-CARE CHECK-IN DAY

How can I partner with God to give myself or receive the support I need?

How do I need to let others know how they can support me today?

DATE / /

Day 38

(Tuesday): Gratitude

Thought for Today

"Give thanks in all circumstances, for this is the will of God in Christ Jesus for you."

(1Thessalonians 5:18, NRSVUE)

The loss of a loved one. A terminal illness diagnosis. Divorce. These circumstances and so many more are a part of the litany of hardships that many people face in this broken world. Then, we read Paul's letter to the Thessalonians and ask, "How am I supposed to 'give thanks' in the midst of this?...This [giving thanks] is God's will for me?"

What we have translated as "give thanks" comes from two Greek words, eu and charis (where we get the word eucharist), which, when put together, quite literally means "good grace."

DATE / /

Day 38

(Tuesday): Gratitude

Thought for Today

With our “I’m fine, and you?” culture in view, I don’t believe that Paul was asking the church (or anyone) to put on a fake mask of happiness when “life is life-ing.” Rather, he was encouraging the church in Thessalonica that in every circumstance, good and challenging, to adopt a posture of always being mindful of God’s good grace. God’s grace that is both good to experience, and that is working for our good, and I’m sure we don’t have to think back too far to recall experiences of God’s good grace in our lives.

Being mindful of God’s good grace can certainly take us to a place of outward expressions of thanksgiving in worship or praise, but quite often, it is simply the spark of hope that gets us through challenging days and what gives us the strength to keep fighting and put one foot in front of the other.

How is God’s good grace ministering to you today?

MY REFLECTIONS

DAY :39 (Wednesday)
SELF-CARE IN ACTION

Create a Gratitude Bank

As a child, did you have a "piggybank" that you saved up coins or money in for a rainy day? As we are concluding this phase of our self-care journey, what better way to do so than by maintaining a discipline of gratitude! To support yourself in this, create a gratitude bank – it can be a box, a special note or running list on your device (iPhone/iPad, etc.), an enclosed home décor item that matches the other items in your home, or any other type of receptacle.

On your Sabbath day at the end of each week, or whenever you desire, take a moment to write down something you are grateful for, and be sure to put the date on it. Then, put it in your gratitude bank. At the end of the year (or on a "rainy day" when you need encouragement), you can go into your bank and celebrate all of the ways that God has blessed you throughout the year!

DAY: 40 (Thursday)

DISCOVERY AND CARE PLANNING DAY

How do you plan to prioritize rest and self-care in your life moving forward?

After journeying through this 40-day experience, I am grateful for:

About the Author

Passionate about education, Jamie is a fourth-generation ordained Christian minister and educator dedicated to providing opportunities for people to learn how to be whole while positively impacting their families, communities, and the world.

Jamie is a graduate of The Johns Hopkins University, Wesley Theological Seminary, and The Catholic University of America, holding undergraduate and graduate degrees in Near Eastern Studies, Divinity, and Biblical Studies.

With over 20 years of experience in ministry, leadership, and education, Jamie specializes in teaching, learning, and leading in ministry and academic settings. She is most fulfilled when she can serve both the academic and church communities.

Jamie is the founder and visionary of Jamie Coles Burnette Ministries, a teaching ministry focused on inviting people into life with God through Jesus Christ and helping them build lives according to Godly principles. She also happily shares her life with her beloved husband, Elliot.

Her life bears witness to the words of Jesus that: "...with God, all things are possible," and she lives daily in gratitude for that being a reality in her life.

Connect with the Author

For bulk purchases, speaking engagements, and/or comments, please connect with me on my social media outlets, email, or website at:

Rev. Jamie Burnette

Soul Sabbath Ministries

Email: hello@soulsabbathliving.love

Ministry Website: www.soulsabbathliving.love